California's topography is characterized by great variety. Its coastline varies from the low, sandy beaches of Southern California to the rocky headlands of Cape Mendocino and other northward protrusions. The Coast Ranges, one of the state's two great mountain systems, runs generally parallel to the coast.

Within the spurs of the Coast Ranges lie many of the state's most fertile agricultural valleys. Eastward is the Central Valley, California's richest agricultural region, which has a width of up to fifty miles. The Central Valley is walled in to the east by the Sierra Nevada rampart, which at Mount Whitney, the highest mountain in the continental United States outside Alaska, reaches an altitude of 14,496 feet.

From the summit of Mount Whitney one can see the weird sink known as Death Valley, 282 feet below sea level, the lowest spot in the United States. Stretching southward are the nation's two largest deserts, the Mojave and the Colorado. By contrast, the topography of northern California contains such large bodies of water as Lake Tahoe and Clear Lake.

7:30-8:00 T

2:30-3:30 T

Hist Final

June 6th   10:30 AM

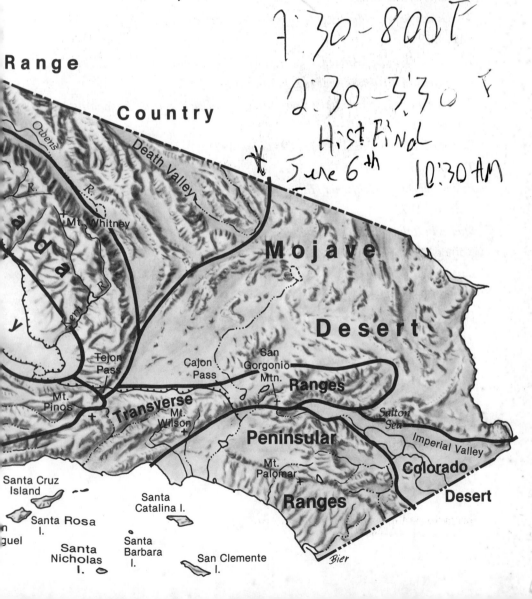

Also by Andrew Rolle

Riviera Path, 1946

An American in California: The Biography of William Heath Davis, 1956

The Road to Virginia City: The Diary of James Knox Polk Miller, 1960

Lincoln: A Contemporary Portrait (with Allan Nevins, Irving Stone, and others), 1961

Occidental: The First Seventy-Five Years, 1962

California: A Student's Guide to Localized History, 1965

Editor of *Helen Hunt Jackson, A Century of Dishonor: The Early Crusade for Indian Reform*, 1965

The Golden State: A History of California, 3rd Ed. (with John Gaines), 1965, 1979, 1990

The Lost Cause: Confederate Exiles in Mexico, 1965, 1990

Los Angeles, A Student's Guide to Localized History, 1965

The Immigrant Upraised: Italian Adventurers and Colonists in an Expanding America, 1968

Editor of *Alfred Robinson, Life in California*, 1971

The American Italians, 1973

Essays and Assays: California History Reconsidered (with George Knoles and others), 1973

Studies in Italian American Social History (with Francesco Cordasco and others), 1975

Los Angeles: The Biography of a City (with John Caughey and others), 1976

Crisis in America (with Allan Weinstein and others), 1977

Perspectives in Italian Immigration and Ethnicity (with Silvano Tomasi and others), 1977

The Italian Americans: Troubled Roots, 1981

Los Angeles: From Pueblo to City of the Future, 2nd Ed., 1981, 1995

Occidental College: A Centennial History, 1987

Henry Mayo Newhall and His Times, 1991

John Charles Frémont: Character as Destiny, 1992